The Danger in Everything

THE DANGER IN EVERYTHING

poems

Jeff Walt

MAD RIVER BOOKS
WINOOSKI, VERMONT

Copyright © 2000 by Jeffery Walt

All rights reserved
Printed in the United States of America

For information about permission to reproduce
selections from this book, write to Permissions,
Mad River Books, PO Box 588, Winooski, VT 05404.

Cover design by BP Design, Burlington, Vermont
Book design by Arrow Graphics, Inc., Cambridge, Massachusetts
Author photograph by Phil Farabaugh

Publisher's Cataloging-in-Publication

Walt, Jeff.
    The danger in everything : poems / Jeff Walt. — 1st ed.
    p. cm.
    LCCN 00-134261
    ISBN 0-9704299-0-8.

    I. Title.

    PS3573.A4715D36 2000   811'.6
    QBI00-901802

Mad River Books, PO Box 588, Winooski, VT 05404
MadRiverBooks@aol.com

AKNOWLEDGMENTS

Grateful acknowledgment is made to the editors of the following journals and anthologies in which some of the poems or earlier versions of them first appeared: *Sahara, The Sun, Bay Windows, RFD, New York Native, The Onion River Review, Christopher Street, The Coastal Forest Review, Out in the Mountains* and *Soulworks*.

"I Was There," "What I Didn't Know," and "Solace, Late in the Day" were included in *Gents, Bad Boys and Barbarians: New Gay Male Poetry* (Alyson Publications, 1995); also "A Game Called Rape," "I Was There," "What I Didn't Know," and "Solace, Late in the Day" were included in *Writing Our Way Out of the Dark: An Anthology by Child Abuse Survivors* (Queen of Swords Press, 1995); "Where We Lived," "The Smell of Sex," "In Transit," and "This World, This Fracture" appeared in *Hard Love: Writings on Violence and Intimacy* (Queen of Swords Press, 1996); "Like Gretel" appeared in *Mourning Our Mothers: Poems About Loss* (Andrew Mountain Press, 1998); some of the poems also appeared in *Passionate Lives*, a chapbook anthology (Queen of Swords Press, 1998); "Coming Together" appeared in *Intimate Kisses: The Poetry of Sexual Pleasure* (New World Library, 2001).

I wish to thank the MacDowell Colony for the fellowship which enabled me to complete this work.

A gracious thank you to my mentors: Linda Tanner Ardison, Elizabeth Claman, Giita Clark, Joe Cosentino, Bob Danner, Mark Doty, Phil Farabaugh, Linda Gregg, Michael Klein, Kurt Leland, Dianna Mitchell, Nora Mitchell, Neil Snook, Jason Stuart Walt and Kahunya Wario.

CONTENTS

What I Didn't Know / 3
Summer Star / 5
The Last Season / 7
Where We Lived / 9
Together All Winter / 11
Evening Voices / 12
Pink / 13
Orogeny / 15
An Empty House After Sleep, After Rain / 17
What Is / 18
What is Given / 20
This World, This Fracture / 21
The Promise / 23
Evenings on Your Back Porch / 25
A Photograph / 27
The Magic / 28
The Discovery / 29
Kitchen Hairdresser / 30
A Common Life / 31
What Remains / 33
Dusk / 34
In Transit / 37
A Game Called Rape / 38
Coming Together / 40
The Smell of Sex / 42
At the Gaslight Laundromat / 43
Late September / 44
I Was There / 45
After Sex / 47

At The Railroad Street Tavern / 49
A Week in the Midwest / 51
Postcards My Brother Used to Send / 52
The Swan / 54
Solace, Late in the Day / 55
All That I've Loved Rushes Back / 56
House of Joy and Rage / 57
Like Gretel / 58
Notes / 60

For

KITTY
my mother, my Moses

Murial,

We are molded and remolded
by those who have loved us,
and though their love may pass,
we are their work, nevertheless,
for good or bad.
—François Mauriac

Jeff Walt
1.7.02

The Danger in Everything

What I Didn't Know

I did not know
what the word *massage* meant
when he said to do it slow.
Nine years of life hide
like a child inside this child;
he touches me through darkness
the way someone will caress
her own image in a pond
to the place where my breasts should have been.
He swirls his fingers like I am ice cream.
His hardness like my hardness, only larger,
like the handlebars of my bike.
His fingers imprint my face
with the graffiti of want.
All the rooms are filled with heavy dreamers,
but they do not dream this.
Massage the thing! he insists.
That word again. What does it mean?
Kiss it. So I do.
I hear the morning paper hit the porch.
I wonder if they'll report
what I've done, if I'll get the electric chair
or gas chamber or prison.
Good girl, he says,
as I crush my face into his ribs
like I think his child might.
I pledge allegiance in my head.
The morning grass is wet.
The sun unfurls.
Birds search for breakfast.
The world is awake.
I know this is the beginning

because the earth has tilted
on her axis to whisper,
This is who you are.

❧

Summer Star

Summer evening.
Fog wanders the yard.
Bats dive and swoop.
We relax on the front porch,
your head on my lap, numb
from good wine and hours of laughter.
I spin the empty bottle
with my foot.
You compare the night
to old film noir—black & white,
mysterious—and convince me
so completely I expect Dietrich
to rise from the shadows
and ask for a light.
We've discussed all that is wrong
in the world, admit
we expected something different
from commitment; we wish
for better pay, long vacations
in the tropics, a winning lottery ticket.
Small frogs leap above the grass.
You undo my trousers with your mouth,
kiss a path to my lips.
A lonely star watches.
We fall to the floor groping
through our clothes, through years
of unmet need, through the alcohol
and guilt. And then nothing.
Like our first drive across Iowa
when you gazed vast emptiness
and questioned: *Why would anyone live here?*
We've traveled to a similar place,

have driven to the Midwest of our hearts.
For minutes we stare at that star's brightness,
and then we begin:
A new wardrobe.
    X-ray vision.
A trip to the Orient.
    A pure bred Golden Retriever.
All the money in the world....

ත

The Last Season

How many summers
have I awakened
to find you beside me, curled
in a fist of sweat and sleep?
How many
restless nights, never dreaming,
wanting someone else
next to you—bars of soap
and plates shared
with a man you hate?
I watched the pond
freeze over and thaw.
Winter.
And winter again.
Frost after frost.
Springs, I wanted
to cut the grass,
but I let it keep growing
(in love with the rain)
until it reached the windows.
I believe the vagrant
who, today, put his dirty face to mine
and said he owns nothing
but one truth:
There is danger in everything.
In this last season
of needing love from you
I am freed by the words
of a simple man
on the street. I don't recall
the exact moment
when I no longer knew the difference

between giving and myself,
but this I know for sure:
I've stopped counting the seasons,
watching the species of birds
that accompany each; drinking
to remember the stranger
drunk enough to undress me
in the back of an old Vega in the dark
parking lot of some dim bar, begging
for words I haven not spoken
in years.

Where We Lived

If I had not looked at myself in the mirror
and seen God instead, maybe I would still be wandering
from room to room in that huge house with a cup
of water, almost drowning the ivy because I was thirsty.

Maybe I'd still be breaking the china, piece by piece,
because I thought you loved the pattern more
than me. Or perhaps I'd reach toward the ceiling
again and grasp the chandelier's hot bulb

until the smell of smoke and flesh suffused the air.
God was everywhere back then.
Wasn't it odd that He came to us?
Like the night I awoke from dreaming about *The End*:

your place next to me in bed was empty and on TV
the Spanish station was playing and there He was
forcing the weatherman's lips, repeating,
¿Como se dice love? *¿Como se dice* love?

I understood his question, understood
how a room can clench like a fist.
I stumbled through fear of being left alone,
through an entire house to the lit kitchen

where not even the wooden table
with its cigarette burns looked familiar.
I said the objects I love most
I do not need, that what should be in my heart

is taped inside a box in the closet.
And in the end—the real end, now—I said,
I am leaving with only the rind of my heart.
The melodrama made us laugh as I backed out the door.

Laughter fell down that dark mahogany staircase.
In the streets I laughed at the common world:
kids lifting a woman's skirt and the wind blowing
a man's toupee into the rain; pigeons cooing *truth*.

My heart began a joyful song
and in the middle suddenly shut up. Laid quiet
for a long while. I did chores with that sad heart.
We lived as people do

inside a frail body without chairs
or a deck of cards for company. We slept
inside our heavy breathing without a wall
to separate us.

ə

Together All Winter

in a small apartment. You
sitting naked on the bed
blowing smoke rings into chains—
I was your devoted audience, begging,
More! More! We ate pudding
from each others fingers. Licked
those tender spots we never dared touch
before. Bought a dog, trained her
to beg and roll over. The twelve steps
together. Your embrace spoke,
No one could love you more.
And then the first drink.
The second. We threw plates,
broke mirrors. No fear of bad luck.
I pulled the fire alarm to call help.
Finally, spring: me standing naked
in the driveway begging you
not to go. Birds sang songs
of loss and joy and life.
And love.

Evening Voices

Mothers call the names
of their children
into the late evening.
Their hard voices echo
in the streets.
We sit on the edge
of the bed after sex,
in the silence
within the silence.
Happy words rush to my lips
but turn back swiftly.
I wish for the past, the days
we lived together and loved.
Remember hours spent wading in
the calm lake? The day you read
forever in my palm? You say
nothing exists beyond our
own breathing in this room,
but I know there is a chest of drawers,
a bureau and lamp, comfort
in the stillness cooled
by dusk's final breaths.
We are startled to hear your name
drift through the window,
some woman calling her son home
for dinner. Your body reacts:
the head lifts, the neck stretches
like that of some frightened bird.
Should you go to her—as if
the voice were your own mother shouting
through years of grief? Quickly
you pull me back onto the dirty sheets,
deep into the rage
of your lips and hands and tongue.

Pink

You were with me those nights
I screamed myself awake to the vacant
landscape of darkness, convinced you had left
for good. *Bad dream, babe?* The reassurance
of your warm breath on my face smoothed the fear.
I'd say I could drink the Niagara.

Without complaint you'd run to the kitchen
for water—5 a.m. and in pink underwear.
I traced your movements as though you were a lit cigarette,
afraid of losing you to the darkness of a room.
And there were nights I'd take you into me
as though one body can enter another and become whole,
like osmosis or simply being eaten alive.
God, we were young—twenty maybe?
You waited tables and I volunteered time at the rehab.
Those were our Renaissance years,

before Florida and herpes and crabs, before
you discovered sex in bathrooms
in department stores at the mall—flesh
pressed against the cold metal stall
and you going down on other men.
That's why I cried for days
after you confessed how being with strangers
was better for you. I got in my car
and drove onto the highway at night
without headlights or caring.
Those were our Dark Ages.

We haven't touched in months, almost
a year of rejection. I wonder if I am ugly?
Do I hunch like Quasimodo in public?

Since pink makes you happy, I buy
bunches of carnations, a pink shower curtain
and rugs to match. Still, you remain distant
and arcane as the constellations,

so I assign names to the years
of our learning, sitting on the edge
of this fountain, children again;
you silent and kicking the water
with an index finger. I want to say,
The End, but prefer the word *prehistoric*.
Our secrets are extinct and now
our life flows into slow decay.

I'll slide into my Victorian years, unable
to lure you back, reel you into the living,
the pink of life. I am the nurse.
I hold a glass of water to your lips at night—
nights you pull me close, a hushed whisper
like confession, pleading: *please, please
let the hearse be fluorescent pink*—a child
or what you really are: convex, a perfect
crescent in sheets, a fragile man pouring
into his thin grave. In heaven, I promise,
you'll be greeted by transvestites with pompoms
and God is just some queen who loves
> neon
> and disco
> and blondes
> and pink
> and pink!

THE DANGER IN EVERYTHING

Orogeny

All day ice breaks from the eaves
in wet, geometric cones—

the plastic covering the windows
slaps heavy breaths of spring against the glass

as the world leans and tilts, shifts
her hips, lifts hills into mountains,

shakes to the song that wakes fossils
from their pre-historic, shale sleep.

Children bake mud pies in the driveway.
They don't know the danger of being

inside a child's body. A lone robin splashes
in the thawing bath in the back yard.

The screen door humps its latch and now
a black dog stares at me from the street.

I am scared. I think the thing is telekinetic
or my father reincarnated.

The kids throw stones and the beast runs
into bushes of burdocks.

They don't know their bikes will rust,
the spokes will bend. Houses can burn.

How the baby in last week's news
was discovered in a dumpster

but still breathing; the way a lamp can slant
a face into the constant, still-weeping hum of regret;

how, even now, the earth's crust is smacking upward,
restless in its bed like a sleeping tyrannosaurus.

Unaware of the orogeny beneath their feet
they go on playing children's games.

Someone could tell them words they've never heard—
touch them into definition,

so that all they might ever notice in spring
is *not* games and *not* playmates,

but the way ice can break all day
from the eaves in wet, geometric cones.

An Empty House After Sleep, After Rain

At dusk, the sun sits
just above the hills
as the shade of the hemlock lies
across my bed. Sunday.
The house is silent.
Chickadees and cardinals praise
the rain. The honeysuckle
seems to have bloomed overnight—
its scent seeps from the windowsill,
explores the room. I am weak
from a day of lifting rocks
from the garden, raking leaves
too wet to burn. All the screens
still in the windows, rain
has sifted in. I do not rush
from these minutes after sleep.
I am listening to the calm pouring
of the spout and thinking
of a friend who says the world
is near its end—love does not exist
and God has left what He created.
I call to my cats, but I am sure
they are asleep, curled deep
in the bathroom hamper.
I hear the back door open and close
and the squeak of wet sneakers
against the kitchen linoleum.
I know that love exists. I know it
like this old house with all its moans
and creaks; like the breeze and the dusk
turning from me; the wet green,
and birds searching for worms
after the rain.

What Is

Heat lightning hovers above the world—
suspended flashes of white
light the face of the earth
brighter than the sun.
I am waiting for the bolts to hit close, zap
the peach tree outside my window,
for the outcry of fire
as it strikes homes, oaks and cattle.
August and fourteen days without rain.
Crickets breed in the weeds and dry grass.
I concentrate, trying to hear the glow
of the moon as she drags
her white train over the streets and rooftops;
watch the ivy and wisteria reach
their miniature fingers over the balustrade.
In the alley, cats dig in the trash, crying,
Want, want, want.
Sirens rush to a house and barn blazing
on the edge of a cornfield.
This could be the end.
I suddenly believe everything
my barber told me just today:
how California is going to plunge
into the Pacific, the way the sun is flickering out
and that the anti-Christ has been born.
I know the bomb could drop tomorrow.
I could be taking the screens out of the windows
for the last time ever as a group of teenage boys
rush to the edge of this city
to feel the fire against their faces,
the way flames can burn you
from a distance, their eyes awed

by something out of control.
They want to know danger,
want to know how close
they can stand to the flames
of a raging fire. I turn away from the blaze,
go into the kitchen, rub an ice cube over my face,
feel my way through this dim house,
wanting to know the darkness
that frightened me as a child.
A night interrupted by cats and sirens and heat.
I don't know if my friend is right.
I don't know who is dying
in that house out there.
Or if we'll get the rain we've prayed for.
I do know it all could be gone before morning—
before the sun slaps the back of my house
with a slab of yellow; before my cat uncurls
into her day of leisure; before my eyes open
to what is and the day rushes to my bed
like a child and I am handed the rumble
of coal trucks passing by, a parade
of second graders guided to a day at the museum.
Lily of the Valley perfumed and flirting
with strangers on the street.

What Is Given

French doors open to the yard
thick with summer light. The father
stands in the doorway whistling
as he slaps raw burgers into shape.
His young son straddles a crooked sand castle,
waves a plastic rake, "Look at me! Look at me!"
The mother applauds, lends an index finger
to her infant daughter starting to walk, learning
her first words, and leads her to the garden,
the perennials: "This is *flower*."
She wants to give her children beauty, a way
to inhale the world. The mother leaps
into the shade of the house: "*shadow*"; then
back into the bright sun: "And this is *light*."
The little girl falls back on her diaper
into the soft grass, laughs hard.
The mother loves the child's disposition.
Loves the man for his strength.
She wants for nothing but the future,
the bouquet of broken daisies pressed
against her daughter's rosy face, the sand
she'll find in her son's cuffs and pockets,
the cool dusk as the sun begins to hem the hills
when she'll pitch an afghan-tent
over all their heads and tell
ghost stories by flashlight, giving them
mystery and plot and darkness:
the dim world that cannot save.

This World, This Fracture

Bev walks the dirt road
her grandmother walked, picks
apples from the trees
her father planted as a boy,

and visits the farmhouse
where her sister-in-law coughs up blood
from her lungs—she is near
the end, so together they reach

into a pocketbook of photos, weave
pain into memory, discuss
first loves, marriage and kids.
They've taken care of each other.

Bev knows this world better
than she knew her husband, his arm
a crowbar across her chest, the all night
games of poker where she played

the barmaid, the whore, *For keeps!*
he'd scream when he ran out of dimes
and quarters. Now she lies awake
listening to the stars, remembering

the son who cried for her at the bus stop
as he makes love to his girlfriend
in the next room. She thinks of the fresh sheets
she put on his bed, the girl's wet center.

She remembers the word *love*,
before the world rose up around her
and fractured. She wants to live.
She wants to sleep in this bed forever;

wants the knock-knock-knock of her son humping,
his headboard bruising the wall.
Her sister-in-law still holding on.
She wants the smell of fresh baked bread

until they smooth the earth over her grave,
the plot beside her husband, down the road,
where she ran from him to her own mother's
tombstone—the graveyard where she played

Doctor and drank beer and sang hymns
in her best Sunday dress; where she listened
to her brother call her name from their childhood
house, her father's belt coiled

around his adult fist,
the steady blows, and that young voice
of her only sibling: shrill as a girl
chased in a game of Tag on the playground,

loud enough to be remembered still,
lunging like a dog where she lay
silent in the wet grass,
the sun and moon framed in the same sky.

The Promise

In 1977 I wore pumps and polyester
bell-bottom pants and danced The Bump
with my sister in our grandmother's living room:
part disco, part asylum.

The malodorous scents of kerosene
and Vick's VapoRub permeated the air.
Curtains, clothes-pinned shut,
brimmed light like silver lining.

We took our skill seriously:
the arduous dance of subterfuge—
away from the blunt edges of our youth.
We wanted our act to become professional,

the best, and make us movie stars:
resonant dreams
as my sister's inordinate beauty
unfolded above old linoleum.

We dedicated our days to
"I Will Survive" and "Hot Stuff"—
angry, invented movements,
grandmother insisting we stop.

We created a new dance step,
The Escape—lucid and fast—practiced
hours in that dark room, my sister lifting me
to the ceiling, the sky if she could,

a slow rotation like the earth.
She was my axis again and again,
perfect stasis, resplendent, cavalier.
I crave the strength

and safety of her slender arms,
and the promise—that divine,
deformed promise—of perfection,
as guide, as torch

through *common* and *stupid*,
through a mother branded *whore*,
to now, where the brilliant light
is dead.

Evenings on Your Back Porch

We talk about sobriety. About
drinking vodka from a suitcase
on vacation at Disney World.
How you punched pillows to release anger—
a month with strangers staring blankly
into childhood. And about now:
a summer evening lit bright
as a birthday cake, your son and daughter
swimming briskly with the dog
in the pool. We bring up the inevitable
subject: mother—amazed she's not dead yet;
agree that her contribution to this world
is sadness. I want to hold you, tell you
how sweet and beautiful you are, but
I don't know how. You yell to the kids:
That's enough, time to come in.
We talk about the lives in Venice
we promised to give each other.
You know you are too young to have a daughter
starting her period, too young for a son
who wants to know about sex, dishes
night after night, a man you wish dead.
Remember the day we stole the Chevy?
Remember thinking we could drive to Europe?
An hour out of town you said we'd better go back
and we did because she'd miss us.
Party's over, time to come in!
Wrapped in beach towels they shiver like dogs,
cross the lawn softly on their toes and rise
to our chairs where they greet us
with trembling, purple lips.
You tell them they are beautiful, and they are,

/ 25

brown and glistening in dusk's final rays.
They joke—laugh hard and loud—go in,
change for dinner. We sit in silence
for minutes. Always wondering
how our lives could have been. Always
forgiving.

☙

THE DANGER IN EVERYTHING

A Photograph

The camera,
arm's length from her face.

She wants to see
what the world sees:

New breasts. Her mother
in her cheekbones. Caretaker.

Her father easing into her bed
at night.

Ten-year-old girl:
the way she came into the world

a lit secret.

The Magic

My niece has reached puberty.
She wants to be a cheerleader, tries out
her best routines for me on the front lawn.
Breasts cupped high; strong legs and muscular arms—
she struts and splits and jiggles to the rhythm
of the music blasting from her boom box.
She already knows about sex, draws pictures
of penises, is very willing to share teenage secrets
that make her mother blush. We are amazed
to hear what she knows about contraceptives, genitals
and syphilis. I struggle to see her as a woman, but
there is only the girl, the child. She practices her cheers,
kicks high above her head, chants: *Be aggressive!*
B-E-A-G-G-R-E-S-S-I-V-E! Boys on bikes cruise by, circle
back, jump curbs, whistle, imitate their fathers' catcalls.
She springs into a series of quick cartwheels
across the lawn—a show off, flirtation in every gesture—
her body naming its desire. She is learning to love
the world. Her charms.
The magic.

The Discovery

My first visit in six years.
Suddenly my sister's son is a man—
sixteen, handsome, learning to drive.
The guest room where I sleep
is next to his. I hear all
the telephone calls, the plan
to deceive his mother,
so he can get to a keg party
by midnight. Music
I've never heard before
and familiar bands like KISS
making comebacks. He tells
his buddies about some girl's tits,
brags, says he got one hand
down her pants. Nightly I listen
to his bed squeak as he thrusts upward
into his adolescent discovery, his cock
in his hand, I imagine, eyes closed
to the fantasy, the adult world
he's dying to enter.

Kitchen Hairdresser

I want to make my mother beautiful,
like a rich woman, so I explain
that the styles of the Sixties are back
as the smell of lilac talcum rises
from between her breasts. She begins
her pregnancy story like I've never heard it:
tells how she was in her eighth month
when Sharon Tate was murdered, says,
Sharon had her unborn cut right out!
All she could think of for days was me,
a fetus inside her and a stranger
using her best knife to dice flesh.
Sick! She insists. *The Sixties were sick!*
I say nothing, just agree to the defamation
of a decade that laid me naked
between her legs without a name.
She refuses a bouffant or simple updo.
A basic cut, short on the sides,
a bit longer on top, and a cold rinse
to close the cuticle. I stand above
my gray-haired mother with dull scissors
I've had since dropping out of cosmetology school.
I want to go deeper into her brain,
a sort of lobotomy to see if she recalls
the past as precisely as I do. *I don't remember*
is her answer to all my questions.
Hairspray makes her choke, so I use care, strive
for even distribution. I've cut more than I should.
She blinks scissor-snips of hair from her lashes.
Her hair clings to my socks like everything
she has forgotten.

A Common Life

> *When you return to something you love,*
> *it's already beyond repair.*
> *You wear it broken.*
> —James L. White

I loved her once, loved
being smothered by her touch, her soft voice
calling me to bed. The men that loved her
are gone, too.

I've never watched anyone die
before, never waited for angels to unleash
their singing, unable to pray for hope
or life; for my mother's suffering.

She twists in misery, reaches
through years of regret, a common life
at its end, presses her frail hand in mine,
begs forgiveness for a life lived wrong.

Some days it seems poetry can be woven
from anything at all: sex, dusk opening
its wings above me, or a mother
on her deathbed trying to say *I love you*

for the first time. I read Cavafy to comfort us:
I do not dare whisper/what I wish to tell you:/
that to live without you/is an unbearable penalty for me…
What kind of bullshit is that? she asks, laughs,

turns from me to her oxygen tank.
she says she's ready to go, ready
for whatever comes next.
I sit in a rocker next to her bed,

begin a slow, contemplative rhythm,
discover comfort in the wild dance she spun in bars,
how she held me in her arms above the lights
of a dusty jukebox, let me pick the songs,

promised me a daddy by midnight.

☙

What Remains

Her piss bucket
under the bed, full
of cigarette butts, mucus,
spit and urine. She couldn't
make it to the toilet, refused
a commode near the end.
I lie on my mother's deathbed,
eyes open to her years
of suffering: the dark apartment,
dreams of the dead whispering
from a shoebox in the closet;
a life of men and drinking curdling
inside—waking without children,
love or youth. A fat Bible
on the nightstand for comfort.
Soiled sheets. Her clipped toenails
scattered on the rug beside the bed.

Dusk

The Lopez brothers—
Casper, Juan, Jose and Jesus—
are working on their father's car.
They yell American obscenities
in thick, Spanish accents,
throw hammers and wrenches in anger,
laugh because they miss each others' heads
by inches. Their mother appears
in the doorway, suds dripping
from her arthritic hands, *Boys, behave!*

I walk past blocks of row houses.
Laundry strung on front porches.
Rap music blares from boom boxes
in second story windows. A man throws
his bruised wife into the streets,
*You want a life? I'll give you a life—
what are you going to do, suck cock for a living?*
Evenings in this ghetto can be full
of noise and clamor, the time of day
when mothers warn their kids
to get off the streets.

I cruise dark corners
as houses begin to light up. Maybe
I should be afraid of the Korean prostitutes
who say they can make sex feel like Heaven.
They give me the finger when I say, *No, thanks*
and yell, *Queer!* once I've passed.

Maybe I should run
as a gang of twelve-year-olds approach

on ten-speeds, call *Shit dick!* and spit
as they peddle by.

There is no silence.
Birds come and go quickly without song.
A baby cries. A car spins its wheels.
Two girls in the street fight over a man
who isn't really a man, but a boy. Kids
tease a dog, beat his back legs with a stick.

Dusk closes its palms above.
Predictable city noise echoes
between the buildings and rises with the heat.
I reach my destination: the dark alley
where men sit in silent cars smoking cigarettes,
waiting for what comes next. Men in tight jeans
rub their cocks as they walk by. Men swaddled
in narrow shadows hold the heads of other men
to their groins like tiny worlds they want
to possess. My life was blessed once at birth
and again in places like this by men calling out
in ecstasy.

I take my place among my comrades, my kin,
lean against an abandoned building and wait,
breathe in the landscape of my heritage
like the poet who rode her horse out at dusk
and wrote,

*And who is to say it is useless/to ride out in the falling
light/alone, wishing, or praying,/for particular good
to particular beings/on one small road in a huge world?*

A truck pulls up
and the guy flicks on his dome light
to show his face, asks if I need a lift.
Yes, I've seen the dark and broken world,
but I still get in. The radio plays
an old love song. He's a cowboy.
Drives with one hand on the wheel
and one on my thigh like I've always been his
and we're on vacation, gone down a wrong alley
by accident in some odd town.

In Transit

Steam rises
from piss—
the tile floor
of a bus station bathroom.
We communicate
like deaf mutes
with simple gestures:
your wink and nod call
me into a rusty stall,
into your corporate after shave,
to my knees.
I am grateful
as you open
the trench coat,
unzip the dark
banker's pants.
Words exchanged
by touch
as I quietly suck
the mystery
from the wellspring
inside you.
You board a bus
for Downingtown
as I wait in transit
knowing
you could never love me
in the bright-lit,
public rooms
of the world.

A Game Called Rape

In my grandmother's living room
my brother and I played
a game called Rape.
We attacked one another

with clenched fists and elbows,
with a hold known as The Claw.
I see my eight-year-old brother
standing half-naked and red in spots;

underwear torn and loose,
thin legs, knees bent and locked,
small testicles showing
like egg-shaped Easter chocolates.

He threatened to crush my skull
and I said I'd cut off his cock
as he beat me against the wall
like a rug full of dust.

When we could go no farther,
we stood back to view the victims—
two lost children left alone—
panting and wondering what came next.

My cousin caught us.
She said we'd grow up and make
perverted real as the Son of God.
Our mother never knew our game.

What I saw and continue to see:
the sexual object of my brother,
flawless, palatable and sweet;
our mimic resurrected,

his head on strangers' bodies
flecked with his freckles.
I am unable to digest his image,
eating entire streets of men.

~

Coming Together

Drenched in summer sweat, I beg,
Wait, don't come yet.
The candle burns to its wick.
The heat and humidity compare
to the intensity of our want:
fire inside and out.
Your face contorts with pleasure—
we know we are near the end, spent,
but still I beg, *Wait for me,*
as I rush to catch up.
My greedy tongue travels your body
like the child I was among the dunes
of the Cape—mysterious, wild, free.
I wonder how the people beyond these walls
can sleep knowing the pleasure
their bodies contain as you scream,
Yes!—More!—Harder!—Faster!—God!
until the moment—like two runners
neck and neck at the end of their race—
I demand *Now!* and we cross
the finish line as one, come together,
trembling, out of breath.
The wick flickers to its end
and the room goes completely black.
I say *I love you*, but already
you are asleep, your wet back turned
to me, so I roll to the opposite side
of the bed, find comfort in the cool
wall as I trace old, dried veins of paint
with my thumb. I do not need
to be next to you to know you love me—

it is in the numb joy of my tongue,
the ache of my hip, the pulse beneath
my nipples that recalls your lips.

ﻋﺐ

The Smell of Sex

I am sure there is a word for this,
but it is not *love*
that glides my hand across his body
like the heart of an Ouija board
pushing toward fate.
The darkness sliced
by the moon's greasy, blue afterglow
smoothes into tight hospital corners
around our slick bodies.
Late August night wets our sex.
I think of how the smell
fertilizes the plums, pulls them
into full bloom so they hang like testicles,
their sweetness like his sweetness
only without the repetition of desire.
The stars blink because the stink
of our sex irritates their eyes,
and bats squawk like children drowning,
swoop from rafters after the smell.
Even the moths that chatter
at the window screen smell our sex
because we are lit from inside
with constant desire. Odd,
I think, to hear kids on the streets.
How can they go on playing
children's games with that smell chasing them?
Especially when just tonight
the plums are coming
into full bloom and sweet desire
has bruised my lips and swells
in my lucky mouth.

ൟ

THE DANGER IN EVERYTHING

At The Gaslight Laundromat

The smell of Tide rises
up from the washer shaking
in its spin cycle. A man
playing pool with a woman
is cursing his last shot.
She gives him the next ball
and he wins, lifts her
with both arms in a bear-hug embrace.
I imagine him an expert
at sex, that she stays
because she loves him.
Because she can endure.
I invent his hardness, assume
the heat between them,
each wanting more
than humanly possible.
I envy the woman for her vagina,
for letting him win the game
of pool. Even after they sit down
at a dirty table—where she feeds
him M & M's, asks him to bark
for each, and he does, then licks
her fingers, kisses her knuckles—
I admire every gesture:
the way she adores his touch,
manipulates the magic of his passion.
Knows how to get what she wants.
His eyes catch mine.
I turn away quickly, fall
into the grace of my need.

Late September

I lie down in a pasture—
harvest begun, the cows'
soft gnawing, headlights
brimming the pines—
to be taken, had.
Hands climb my ribs.
My tongue and hipbone
recall the joy:
the clover and heifer
and mist; the night
owl calling. The sky's
hundred eyes shine down.

ଌ

I Was There

I was there when you turned five
unable to ride a bicycle
like your sister did at that age,
training wheels until you were seven,
playing with matches, dressing
in girls' clothes, applying make-up
to your eyes and cheekbones,
a gypsy: you prayed for a vagina,
wished upon the stars that freckled the sky.

At nine, neighbors got you drunk
and dancing naked on the kitchen table.
Disco became air you inhaled—
unable to live without it—
while someone flashed the kitchen light
off and on, until you were too tired
and someone older carried you off
like an infant to the bedroom
up the stairs and down the hall:
where each took a turn teaching
you, as they said, to love.

When ten years of life spilled
into your body, you were seduced
by a forty-year-old man
who thought he'd try and score
with your mother. Drunk
that night, passed out, she talked
to herself in the next room
while you licked the genitals
of a stranger: hairier and bigger
than yourself.

Twenty years have brought you here:
sitting complacent, a leather chair
molding beneath you, the smell of violets
coming from somewhere, explaining guilt
to Dr. Puckett: you wanted the sex,
even then, to fill the empty bivouac
of your heart. I was there with you,
and now you reside safely inside of me, dressed
in knee-torn jeans, red cheeks, balancing
on railroad tracks, arms extended,
not even falling off. They all want
to touch you, but they can't,
now that I won't allow it.

After Sex

he *must* shower, *has* to,
so I grip his love handles
and he guides me through darkness
to the bathroom's small light.
He needs to scrub the lust—
the smell of sex, come, hours
of going at it—from his body.
Past midnight and I sit
on the toilet wanting come
and sweat and cologne greased
over me like a thin membrane
as a reminder, a token.
I want to wake with it on me.
Want it forever.
Winter knocks at the window.
Eyes closed and shivering,
I relax for minutes
after I've finished, drift
toward sleep, calculate
bills, build my dream house
in my head, remember
how I turned onto Rt. 2 yesterday
and swerved an S from a truck
driving in the wrong lane.
I went to work, baked bread,
held the soft loaves like babies
to my make-believe breasts.
I knew I could be dead, I knew
they'd use the Jaws of Life
to pry the steering column
from my chest.
He leaps from the shower,

kisses my forehead—
Who loves ya, baby?—
runs wet to the bed
and without drying off
jumps under the covers.
I want to say nothing
can ever hurt me badly again—
not love nor death nor living—
but I know it's not true; yet
I want no other life than this.
I flush the toilet, tell myself:
This is romance, baby! and run—
swiftly, tip-toed—
from the night-light's soft glare
to the bed and curl deep
into the moist comfort
of the body I know like my own.

At the Railroad Street Tavern

In this small town
we sit mutely at the Railroad Street Tavern,
years of questioning commitment between us,
cobalt blue neon flashing on our faces.
We scan cracks in the ceiling and walls, recognize
disfigured creatures and villains from our youth
reaching out—Godzilla and Mothra doing battle;
Darth Vader's dark face. Your profile
resembles the bust of Neffertiti,
which my university professor describes as
The most beautiful artifact in western civilization.

In 1978 I spent five dollars in quarters
playing disco music and Loretta Lynn for mother.
The dusty jukebox now a dying animal hunched
in the corner. *"Franny '75"* is inscribed
on my bar stool: she stripped here back then
to pay the rent, a tavern star, my mother's friend.
I remember her blue G-string, pink tits pointing—
men stretched for them as though a simple touch
could restore their youth. I ate cashews
and sat Indian Style on the floor, docile
beneath the masculine chant, *More, more, more!*
Franny let me sleep in her bed once when I was five.
She read *Charlotte's Web*, and in the end when the spider died,
she wept. I didn't understand.

I exaggerate stories of my fictitious life in New York
to vagrants and drunks who remember me
as a skinny kid—welfare mothers and winos
who appeased my childhood, barroom complaints
with spare change. They gape, glossy stares, worshipful

as a cult. I am a good liar, and they believe
everything I say.

The sky is dull. Autumn's murky Susquehanna water
slaps upward, pinching cold. Neglected children slide
down the muddy banks and throw stones at ducks
who think they are being fed—the exact spot
where Franny's body was fished out, soaked
for days after a drunken August swim.

I hear the river from our seats in the bar.
You say I am crazy. Your neck is long and slender.
I loved you once.
Across the room a silver-haired man yells, *Hey,
maybe I'll win the lottery and buy this whole fuckin' town.*
You laugh. I'm as far away as the words
I need to say, remembering only this:

summer night,
Franny and mother braided together, falling
into the canticles of love-making, vows exchanged
by touch; the bedroom swallowed by the moon's tender
blue, and the three of us—two women in ecstasy
and a boy spying from behind a closet door—believing
what the moment whispered of passion and joy.
Grief wrung temporarily from our hearts.

જ

THE DANGER IN EVERYTHING

A Week in the Midwest

We sat on the patio
for a week
like tourists watching
for lightning, a tornado
or storm. But they
never came. Instead,
there was just us
learning to use
the *right* words, naming
our feelings,
placing no blame.
We passed happiness
back and forth
like an adored, only child.
Nights without
even a star falling. Nights
of us talking softly,
laughing about the time
we tried to throw
each other down
a silent staircase.

Postcards My Brother Used to Send

I found the poetry and postcards
my brother sent me,
buried in a shoebox beneath the calm,
yellow chill of antiquity.

The skyscrapers and boardwalks
he called home rise to view
in my palm—torn and wrinkled
panoramic sights of city streets:

Castro, Christopher, Bleecker, Duval—
"Full," he wrote, "yet so empty."
I shuffle his happiness
in my hands: still-lifes

of his errant ways scattered before me.
I see him smile in each.
He never called home.
They adored him in neon-drenched cities

where, I know, men dance on pillars
in pink light, tight underwear,
laser beams growing
into their chiseled torsos.

His poetry confused me: childhood,
masturbation, men together in bed.
Now his life is a blur on my carpet:
"Sis, you must come to New Orleans—

you'd love the French Quarter!"
I live an ordinary life here in Iowa
and my children will grow up
never knowing their lost uncle, going

slowly as I scrub the drawers of my hutch:
a complete resurrection and burial at once
for the boy whose peregrinations
became his family. The last postcard

from Boston, barely legible, inscribed:
"It was the only life I had."–melodramatic,
a quote from a poem. The wake is tomorrow,
someplace Northeast, his remains blown

on winter snow, freezing until spring
when he'll grow into daffodils and azaleas,
second life, *true* beauty, reaching toward
the sun in daylight and the moon, safe moon.

The Swan

I was alone after he died,
but I am not lonely.

What pity they must've felt,
knowing there were only
the two of us,

assuming me female,
admiring my slender neck,
Wings like an angel! children exclaim.

I begin my life again
without a cob
or cygnets to ride my back,

yet all about this soft marsh
there is assurance:

Love never leaves you, really.

It is there: in the bulrushes
and horsetails, water lily, reeds.

And here: in the muskrat
and dragonfly and king snake,

inside me and out.

ಣ

Solace, Late in the Day

Today I loved my dog's sour breath.
His tongue entered my mouth by accident
and it wasn't so bad. I loved
the smell of radish under my fingernails
and the headless Barbie Doll
a child must've buried in my garden.
I love my muffler that drags
and the holes in my underwear; the way
my skin wrinkles around my eyes
when I smile, and my sore hip
that gives away my age. I love
this damp house that smells
of Windex and Pledge, how I carefully
smoothed the fine mahogany
of the coffee table, held the knobbed spine
of the rocker the way I did my first lover
with so much precision. I loved
my bath water that went cold
this afternoon as the last slab of pink
broke from the sky like slate
as God crawled onto the window sill
with the breeze and watched me
dry off. He came to me without
light, without vision or wings, without
contradiction: He left me with my life
around me and I kept it.

All That I've Loved Rushes Back

Every Friday night I sit with a friend
on his front porch, watch the hectic streets
of this college town, discuss rage and lust,
how, near forty, we suddenly feel old.
Tonight, the autumn moon blooms red.
A group of young men with Greek letters
painted on their chests howl at the sky
like a pack of wolves as they run past.
School is back in session. The liquor store
across the street is busy. Cars pulse and thud
with music we can't understand.
A young couple walks by hand-in-hand, stops,
pulls each other into a forgiving embrace,
French kiss, move on. Suddenly, I ache
for the old days, the warm joy of another
person's tongue, for the splendor of smoothing
a stranger's come over my stomach and thighs.
The strobes and blue lights and disco balls
of dusty bars. Drag queens wrapped in sequins—
songs torched by their tragic hearts. Men
who made sex feel like my first time over and over
again. How I slept so entwined with my first love's body
that I once mistook his leg for mine gone numb. Tonight,
all that I've loved rushes back to me, sings its song
with such passion that I want to croon along, unzip
my aging skin and dance with a man whispering
I love you in a room full of smoke and bad language, comfort
in the sad joy of knowing he'll excuse himself after sex
and I may never—in my entire life—see him again.

House of Joy and Rage

The bald moon still
in the sky this morning.
The road to the house is mud.
Rain for days. Arabesques
of dead moss cling to the bark
of the bare oak. All the leaves
gone from the trees. The fog
near the barn creeps to the fields.
I've learned to cherish the familiar:
the pond black and ominous,
the lichened bridge rotting,
a cluster of siskins and goldfinches
travelling together gather
in the pines, how, last night,
I dreamt you beside me and awoke
to realize—again—that you left.
Gone years now. The horses
recognize my voice, the sloshing
of my boots, the scoop in the feed.
They whinny. I lead the blind male
to the field; his muddy eyes open
even when he sleeps. He knows
my touch, trusts it. The others
trot, race, then take a place
near the fence. I see my home
hunched in the distance: a plain house
warm with joy and rage and memory.
First love of my middle age.

Like Gretel

I wanted to be the first
to go. Not the strong one
left behind squinting
away winter light,
scattering ashes blessed
with prayers I do not understand—
handfuls of you
on the wet snow. And me,
like Gretel looking back
at the trail of ash, my tracks
following me deeper
into the dark wood.

NOTES

The quote in the poem, "A Common Life," P. 31, is taken from C. P. Cavafy's poem, "Had You Loved Me," from *The Complete Poems of Cavafy*, translated by Rae Dalven, Harcourt, Brace, Jovanovich, Inc., 1976.

The quote in the poem, "Dusk," P. 35, is taken from Linda McCarriston's poem, "Riding Out at Evening," from her book, *Talking Soft Dutch*, Texas Tech Press, 1984.

The quote in the poem, "Postcards My Brother Used to Send," on P. 52, is taken from Jane Kenyon's poem, "Three Songs at the End of Summer," from her book, *Let Evening Come*, Graywolf Press, 1990.